BRIGHT
IDEA
BOOKS

CHADWICK
Boseman

by Aubrey Zalewski

D1335961

Raintree is an imprint of Capstone Global Library Limited, a company incorporated in England
and Wales having its registered office at 264 Banbury Road, Oxford, OX2 ?DY - Registered
company number: 6695582

www.raintree.co.uk
myorders@raintree.co.uk

Edited by Claire Vanden Branden
Designed by Becky Daum
Original illustrations © Capstone Global Library Limited 2020
Production by Melissa Martin
Originated by Capstone Global Library Limited
Printed and bound in India. PO 864

ISBN 978 1 4747 8742 0

British Library Cataloguing in Publication Data
A full catalogue record for this book is available from the British Library

Acknowledgements
Alamy: D. Stevens/Universal Pictures/Photo 12, 18–19, Fox Studios/Entertainment Pictures,
14–15, Marvel Studios/Entertainment Pictures, 24–25; AP Images: Evan Agostini/Invision, cover;
Rex Features: Legendary Pictures/Kobal, 17, Michael Buckner/Variety, 21; Shutterstock Images:
Featureflash Photo Agency, 5, 28, 31, Kathy Hutchins, 9, 11, Pawika Tongtavee, 12–13, Sarunyu L,
6–7, Tinseltown, 23, 26–27
Design Elements: Shutterstock Images

Every effort has been made to contact copyright holders of material reproduced in this book. Any
omissions will be rectified in subsequent printings if notice is given to the publisher.

All the internet addresses (URLs) given in this book were valid at the time of going to press.
However, due to the dynamic nature of the internet, some addresses may have changed, or sites
may have changed or ceased to exist since publication. While the author and publisher regret any
inconvenience this may cause readers, no responsibility for any such changes can be accepted by
either the author or the publisher.

CONTENTS

CHAPTER 1

A REAL
Hero

The crowd cheered. Chadwick Boseman walked onto the stage. He put his hand to his chest. He took a deep breath. He had just won an award for Best Performance in a Movie.

Boseman won the award for playing King T'Challa in *Black Panther.* His character was the superhero Black Panther. It was the first Marvel film with a mostly black **cast**. Boseman thanked the other actors in his speech. He said he could not have been a good hero without them.

Chadwick Boseman won Best Performance in a Movie at the 2018 MTV Movie & TV Awards.

Boseman is a hero in films. But he also knows how to be one in real life. In 2018 Boseman visited sick children at St Jude Children's Research Hospital in Memphis, Tennessee, USA. He spent time with the kids. They had a chance to meet a real superhero. Boseman wants to use his fame to help others.

Many children look up to superheroes such as Black Panther.

CHAPTER 2

FINDING
His Talents

Chadwick Boseman was born on 29 November 1977. He grew up in South Carolina, USA.

Boseman enjoyed stories when he was little. His brother liked to dance and act. Boseman would watch him in plays. Boseman liked the way plays told stories but he did not want to act.

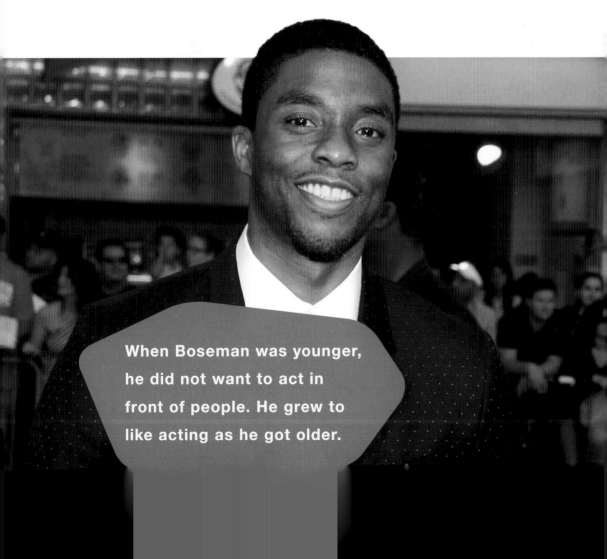

When Boseman was younger, he did not want to act in front of people. He grew to like acting as he got older.

Boseman played basketball at school. One day one of his teammates was shot and died. Boseman was very sad. He wrote a play to help with his feelings. He performed the play in front of others. This made him realize that he wanted to write and **direct** plays.

Boseman knew that he wanted to work in the **performing arts.**

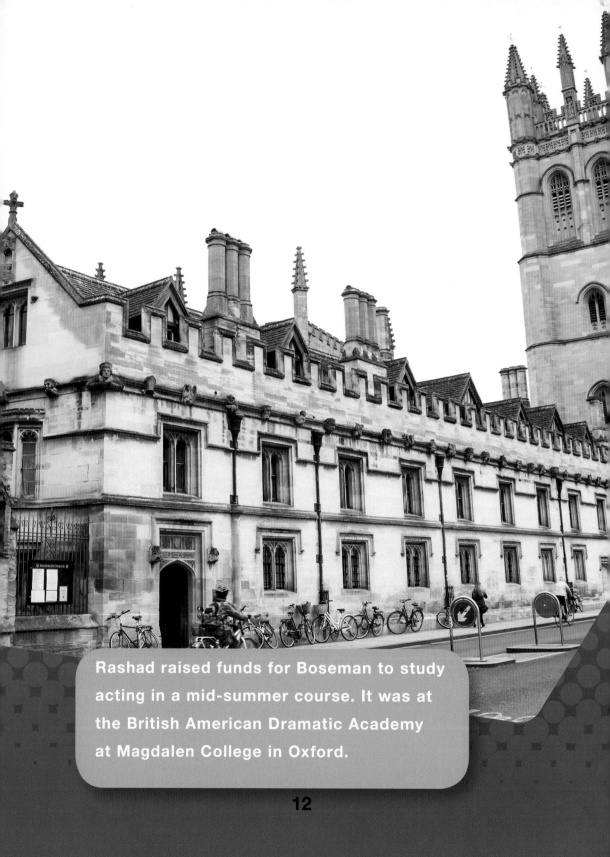

Rashad raised funds for Boseman to study acting in a mid-summer course. It was at the British American Dramatic Academy at Magdalen College in Oxford.

COLLEGE YEARS

After high school Boseman went to Howard University in Washington DC. He studied directing. One of his teachers was the well-known actress Phylicia Rashad, who encouraged him. Boseman wanted to be a good director. So he had to learn how to act. He needed to know how actors worked. He needed to know how to talk to them. These **skills** would help him be a good director.

Boseman began to like acting. But he still wanted to direct. Boseman stuck to his dream. He wrote plays and did some directing. He also acted on TV shows. Soon Boseman would act in films.

Boseman went from acting in small parts on television to having bigger parts in films. In 2016 he played Thoth in *Gods of Egypt.*

CHAPTER 3

SHARING
Important Stories

In 2013 Boseman got his first big part. He starred in the movie *42.* He played Jackie Robinson. Robinson was a famous baseball player. He was the first black baseball player in the US major leagues in the 20th century.

Boseman had to practise his baseball skills for the role of Jackie Robinson.

Boseman learned many kinds of dances when playing James Brown.

Boseman was in many films after that. He played James Brown in *Get on Up* in 2014. Brown was a musician. He was an early performer of the music style **funk**. He is known as "the Godfather of Soul".

JAMES BROWN

Boseman had to play James Brown perfectly. He needed to dance and sing just like Brown. Many people loved Brown so Boseman was afraid he would get it wrong. He almost did not take the part. But he wanted the challenge.

In 2017 Boseman starred in *Marshall*. He played Thurgood Marshall. Marshall was the first black Justice (judge) of the US Supreme Court. That is the highest court in America.

Boseman has played important people in films. He wants to share their stories. Boseman thinks there should be more movies about black people. He has said many of their stories have not been told.

Boseman is famous around the world.

CHAPTER 4

A DIFFERENT
Part

In 2018 Boseman's life changed forever. He starred in *Black Panther.* The film showed parts of many different African cultures.

The film was a huge hit. It was **nominated** for seven Academy Awards (known as Oscars) in 2019. These awards are given to the best films in the world.

Boseman attended the 2019 Academy Awards, where *Black Panther* won three awards.

BLACK PANTHER

The part of King T'Challa as Black Panther was different for Boseman. He was not playing a real person. But Boseman believes his part as T'Challa was just as important as other parts he had played. The film covered real problems in the world.

BIG SUCCESS

Black Panther broke many box office records. It made $242 million (£200 million) in its first weekend in cinemas. It has made more than £1 billion around the world.

In *Black Panther*, King T'Challa rules the fictional country of Wakanda.

Boseman wants to continue to take roles that tell black people's stories.

Black Panther was very popular. Boseman wants to make films with black characters more popular worldwide. *Black Panther* was a huge success. But Boseman says there is more work to be done.

GLOSSARY

cast
the people who have parts in a film, play or TV show

culture
the ideas and practices of a group of people

direct
to lead the actors and stage crew in a film, play or TV show

nominate
to suggest that a person might be the right one for a job or an award

performing arts
creative activities that are performed in front of an audience

skill
an ability to do something well

TIMELINE

1977: Chadwick Boseman is born in South Carolina, USA.

2000: Boseman graduates from Howard University in Washington DC with a degree in directing.

2013: Boseman stars in the film *42*.

2014: *Get on Up* is shown in cinemas.

2017: Boseman stars as Thurgood Marshall in *Marshall*.

2018: Boseman stars in *Black Panther* as King T'Challa, the Black Panther.

ACTIVITY

WRITE AND DIRECT A PLAY

Chadwick Boseman wrote plays before he acted. Try writing your own play. It could be based on your life or it could be completely made up. Pick a topic that is important to you. After you have written your play, ask your friends to act it out. You can direct them or even act with them. Perform your play for an audience.

FIND OUT MORE

Want to know more about important people in black history? Take a look at these resources:

Books

28 Days: Moments in Black History that Changed the World, Charles R. Smith (Roaring Brook Press, 2015)

Little Leaders: Bold Women in Black History, Vashti Harrison (Puffin, 2018)

Young, Gifted and Black: Meet 52 Black Heroes from Past and Present, Jamia Wilson (Wide Eyed Editions, 2018)

Website

Fun facts about black American actors:
fun-facts.org.uk/black-americans/black-american-actors.htm

INDEX